MUCH

by
Joel Peckham

UnCollected Press

MUCH
Copyright © 2021 by Joel Peckham

All rights reserved. This book in full form may not be used or reproduced by electronic or mechanical means without permission in writing from the author and UnCollected Press.

Cover Art:
>Lily Jurskis
>***God's Bicycle***
>mixed media

Book Design by:

UnCollected Press
8320 Main Street, 2nd Floor
Ellicott City, MD 21043

For more books by UnCollected Press:
www.therawartreview.com

First Edition 2021
ISBN: [ISBN]

Table of Contents

I. WARNING SIGNS 1

    On Hearing a Scream Outside My Window 3

    Warning Signs 5

    The Boy and the Bell Rope 7

    Trembling Into Winter 8

    Redemption Center 9

    Donnie Russo and the Huffy Pro Thunder 10

    Some Crazy-Ass Shit 12

    Pavement: Jack Coffey Landscaping and Tree Service, July 1989 15

    You don't know shit about shit 16

    Much 17

    Barn-light 19

II. INTO THE TEETH OF THE WIND 21

    Jupiter, Desire, Hope 23

    #naturalselection 25

    Night Patrol—Batavia Ohio 27

    America: Love It or Leave It 29

    Burning Down The Cathedral 31

    Catch and Release 32

    Sometimes I'd Forget 34

    In the moment where I decide there must be a God because 36

    Wow! Signal: Dredging Light 37

I. WARNING SIGNS

On Hearing a Scream Outside My Window

1.
A crying not to but through, entering just below the ribs, then the soft tissue
    of the world, its muscle and sinew, and out
the back, like a bullet—into the swell of the street rising to meet her and
    absorb her just beyond my sight or memory or
hope in a heat-shimmer of tarry pools—the light playing a trick with the eyes
    and the way the mind desperately pieces things together, trying to
follow the track as it bends into woods, imposing patterns, asking all the
    leading questions—like
what or why or who and how soon or where did she go because everything
    must have a destination
and a source. So all day I imagined and reimagined the voice

of the great grandmother I never knew, the one my sisters feared, who, in
    her last years would spend thanksgiving screaming that her husband
    was trying
to kill her, tearing at her hair and weeping in terror as everyone shook their
    heads, staring at their drinks—*you don't know what you don't know
    you don't know
what you think you know.* Her voice the voice of the wild god of snake
    venom and tongues where everything and everyone is the holy ghost
    announcing the Pentecost. So

each cry is a mortar, a flaming arrow, a ball that rises out of the park and
    keeps going up and over—the note that hovers and lingers long after
    the singer
has run out of breath. The silence of remission, of the space between the one
    who screams and the one, head down, hands folded, forced
to listen.

2.
As a boy I would spin my mother's old records on the stereo credenza in the
 living room and try to understand how John Lennon
was gone when I could hear him right there in the room, echoing
in oak. Easier to believe in the death of God than the death of John crying
Help and *Power* and *Mother* until I heard his voice split
Once, then twice, then three times (and a fourth that might have been
George and Paul, or even Yoko harmonizing) and it was all
for me and through me—those cries I heard and those I hadn't yet heard or
 would make myself
in time. Years later. Now,

I often wonder if Lennon, like Oppenheimer blinded by the spreading cloud
of fire as it rose, was ever afraid
of what he'd done. This terror turned to beauty. This force
freed from the sun.

Warning Signs

When we speak of "safe" and "unsafe" as more than signs shaken by the
    wind—how they might be
a kind of ward, a warning, a benediction granted if we could hang them in a
    classroom or an alleyway or from
the one streetlamp blooming in the parking lot across 5th avenue, I think of
    the signs I saw as a boy in fields
behind my house: "Danger!" "Warning!" "Violators

Will Be Prosecuted!" And how I would step over or between them, fishing
    pole and net in hand, taking the shortcut
along the electrical towers to the glacial pond surrounded by scrub-oak and
    pine—one end
of a rope tied to a thick branch arced lazily above dark water in sunlight. The
    other wrapped around another sign: "No
Swimming!" Because a word can seem reality, a fist when it is only a child's
    sketch of a hand. Because a sign
can only seem—is halfway, in-between, slippery, and

that's its power. Sometimes we'd sit, stripped, dripping on the banks and tell
    each other stories of a body found
floating, having somehow worked its way from whatever the killer had tied
    around its feet and swum up, shoeless
sexless, bloated beyond description, recognition, and we'd shiver, blue lips
    quivering. Sometimes the thought that we
are fragile— in body, in spirit—is thrilling. And strength

a kind of body-language. The abdomen tightening, a flexed calf, a lip curled
    up in the ecstasy
of a scream, as the body flies up and out, mirrored over water for an instant,
stopped mid-air with the contrails and the clouds and the hawk, before
    gravity, before *make sure you're home before*
Dinner. Or what? *Or else*. But jogging, sprinting anyway,

spooled out of and into a lengthening shadow. Before consequences. Knowing there are consequences, especially
when there aren't. Angler, swimmer, flier if I could only weave the words that
       would protect you, I would

not— because this sign around my neck that says "safe" might also read as

"warning" that you never were or are.

The Boy and the Bell Rope

rising from the ground does not make but initiates the sound, and we are
 carried off. Somewhere

in the chest-deep cages of its bones, the whole town rings itself awake, aloft,
 shudders like an ocean.

Trembling Into Winter

The quaking aspen spins its gold to daybreak all along the path above the park, and
    sets the world alight, shivery
with flame. And once again I'm barreling through the path above the bogs at high
    speed reckless with my friends, chasing each other
on bikes that flash like sparks though wool, our thighs and calves still hot with blood,
    chins tucked down
into the chill and all of us hollering ahead and behind, *Wait up. Come on. Get the
    lead out lard-ass.* Scaring
sparrows into flight as tires skip and slip on slick mud over stone and fingers turn
    numb on handlebars. Once we found
a suit spread out by a tree near a pond. Navy blue with pin stripes. There was

a starched white shirt and tie folded by the trunk. As if someone had walked out of
    a bank or some
cubicle in one of the office parks and crossed through traffic by foot. Or maybe
    pulled his car into the breakdown
lane off 95 and walked up the embankment into the woods, undressing as he went,
    folding the jacket over an arm, unloosening first the tie and then the belt.
    Wait. What happened
to the shoes? We looked around, half expecting one of our fathers to step out from
    behind
an oak, dressed only in his boxers and a pair of loafers:

Boo! Pete pushed at the pants with a stick. Neil said, *don't touch anything*—as if we
    would or could. I perched, one foot
on a pedal. One foot on the ground. Ready

to bolt.

Redemption Center

I remember hunting soda cans along the edges of the strip mall parking lot, fingers sticky with sugar and oil, turning shades of black and orange as I tipped hot syrup into a hissing puddle on the blacktop. *Five cents a "pop"* the huge sweating man behind the counter liked to say, cheeks shaking at the pun. But it was no joke as I leaned into the counter, waiting for him to count them up—I always knew I'd need to get my hands a little dirty to get what I wanted. And what did I care if a schoolmate cruising past in the plush velvet of his father's Continental pointed and laughed at my garbage bags and dirty jeans, my t-shirt stained with grease and filth? Two hundred cans. Ten bucks. Just enough for a movie ticket and popcorn. Sometimes I still long for it— the simple return, when the deep dive of a theater on a sweaty summer afternoon and my head, swimming in the cool dark, seemed all the compensation I could ever need, and all I could afford.

Donnie Russo and the Huffy Pro Thunder

You know anything about this, my father asked, *anything at all?* And I remember it like a punch in the gut—a Huffy BMX Pro Thunder: red and white with a long banana seat and deep padded V in the handle bars, designed to look like it begged to be ridden too fast down dirt roads but still somehow trying too hard to look mean and slick so even when I slid to a halt spraying stones as I jammed the peddle back, pulling to the right, leaning into the skid, it only made the chubby kid riding it seem chubbier. Still, it might as well have been a rocket-ship to me, and I remember the despair of having to tell my father it was gone from the grass by the driveway where I'd dropped it on its side before running into the house, trying to beat the sun on a summer Friday evening and *yes I looked everywhere*. And *no it's not in the shed*. And *no it's not leaning against the house. It's gone.* And so here was Dad staring Donnie down, the older kid my father called a punk who once tried to teach me how to pop a wheelie in his driveway, though I couldn't get the balance right, front wheel coming up only a few inches from the ground with a timid tug so his friends laughed and shouted *he can't get it up* or I yanked the handle bars too hard too far and leaning back, went past the tipping point to land on my ass so that they laughed even harder until he gave up in disgust. I made myself as small

as possible, listening, peeking up through my eyelids as Donnie's friends stared away or at the ground, acting like a group of slightly smaller, uglier, Donnies, trying to look casual in the heat of that day and the presence of a man they feared and hated and loved. And Donnie, unblinking, returning my father's gaze. *I might have an idea. Maybe.* Which was as good as saying, *yeah, I know where it is,* as good as saying, *I can get it back if I feel like it.* And my dad saying nothing but nodding hard once and turning his back and walking past me into the house like *that was that* like *problem solved.* And Donnie saying, *you just wait here JoJo.* And so I spent that Saturday morning on that stoop staring at the tops of my shoes, waiting and thinking about Donnie and his pack of friends peddling off like they were the Lincoln County Regulators on dirt-bikes and Donnie was Billie the Kid staring some greasy punk down, arms akimbo, saying *how do you want to do this*. And this other kid

staring back at Donnie and his friends behind him, knowing he was beat and there was nothing to do and nowhere to run that was far enough. *You just give me the bike and we'll pretend this never happened.* And he could have been Clint or Carradine, biting down on a half-smoked cigar. Still I want to imagine him like that, standing in silhouette—hair glued back with Aquanet, smelling of Drakkar Noir and sweat, but itching for that kid to say something, do anything. And sure enough, just past high noon, he appeared, tearing down the dirt road, kicking up the dust, front wheel aloft, radiant atop a bike that was mine and not mine and never could or would be—spray-painted black with a saddle seat. The padding gone, the deep V handlebar replaced by something simple and squared off as a shotgun and as much a part of Donnie as his worn black Chucks. I only rode it couple of times after that and I can't remember if we gave it away or sold it or dropped it off at the dump. I had a birthday coming and got a bright blue 10-speed and a paper route. But the next time my dad called Donnie a punk, it stung and I spoke up, *Hey dad, c'mon. He got my bike back for me. Remember?*

"*Returned it*" *you mean.* He laughed and shook his head, staring back for a second like he couldn't quite believe I was his son. *You mean to say, it's been this long and you haven't figured that out?*

Some Crazy-Ass Shit

That was some crazy-ass shit Pete said, eyes wide in wonder, cheeks aflame, his thick frame padded to absurdity in scarves and coats emblazoned with the names of his favorite teams—Patriots, Bruins, Celtics, Sox— two sweatshirts and two pairs of sweatpants over jeans. It was cold and wet but our bodies steamed up with our breath above us

as we hooted and laughed and peeled little Robbie Russo up from the slush of dirt and snow where he finally slid and came to a halt twenty feet from the ramp we built into the side of the hill as his little sister Charlene's pink boots chased a saucer-sled across what could have been the surface of the moon in the field behind the K-Mart parking lot where route 95 split Main and Mechanic. It seemed

the closer you lived to the sounds of the highway and the trains, the farther from the center of the town and the lake and the bird streets where rich kids "played" on tennis courts in pools and batting cages in their back-yards, the crazier you were, the more likely to talk the McMullen kids into lying down in a row at the end of their driveway, laughing and screaming so you could pedal your huffy flying up a plank of wood and into the air, Evel Knievel jumping the fountain at Caesars Palace, the more likely to break

your coccyx or your nose or your thumb or show up to school with mystery bruises all over your body so your mom got a call home from the middle-school guidance counselor threatening a visit from child protective services and you'd have to spend the next two weeks grounded while everyone else got to play touch football and shoot bb guns at cans over at Pete's house. None of us were the kids most likely to do anything

of consequence. And we were all a little afraid of each other's fathers (who our fathers could beat the shit out of any day of the week). Afraid of how they'd fight with our mothers at night when we were trying to

sleep, shouting and punching walls until they left the house, peeling
down the driveway, and how

we wondered if they'd come back and wondered how we felt about that. And
how everyone shoveled in their Lucky Charms the next day at the
kitchen table as if nothing out of the ordinary had happened because
nothing had as Mom

told your sister to go wash that crap off her face or she wouldn't let her on
the bus. And that's not even the crazy part. The crazy part was, we
never really were all that afraid. Fear was just

what you added to make things interesting and strange like something Pete's
gypsy grandma sprinkled pungent in the stew as we drank Milk-and-
Pepsis watching Death Race 2000 in the living room. Otherwise, you'd
just mark your distance with a piece of sidewalk chalk. Otherwise,
what's the point?

of believing in marriages and bones that would bend not break or at least
would heal,

believing that there was nothing you couldn't rise up from or to if you were
tough and lucky,

believing that divorces, depression, and cocaine were problems for rich
people, and

that too much money came with too much trouble,
that you slept better in a cold house,
that the mafia killed Kennedy,
and you can't get pregnant the first time,
and in an angry but forgiving God,
in *holy fuck that was awesome, let's do it again,*
and faster and higher
and farther,

and the Clash and the Ramones and how much Bon Jovi sucked (though we all sang along for Tommy and Gina, holding on)

and driving reckless on a dirt road in a rebuilt Gremlin, the car getting air to the strains of "Mama Kin," then fishtailing behind you, throwing up stones, as Charlene laughed and Robbie prayed, alive, alight in the belief

that you might as well take a running start and scream away the dark,

in flying and falling and flying again, heaven and hell, and more than a little

crazy-ass shit.

Pavement: Jack Coffey Landscaping and Tree Service, July 1989

He said we were going to do it anyway and do it now. He had a steaming heap of asphalt in the bed already and though the sun was hot in a clear blue summer sky so humid you felt greased and loose he felt in his shoulders the pressure of coming rain. It wouldn't, couldn't wait or we'd lose the day. Lose the heat, the job and that stinking slurry of oil and stone and sand would cool and harden to a crust and then what? *This is gonna suck,* Joey Fontez said. *Man oh Man. Jesus Fucking Christ,* pulling on his gloves, tying his bandana around his face. As Jack's sister Lisa smoked her cigarette, grunted, and shook her head—mumbling something beneath her breath. The chutes had failed to rise no matter how much muscle or violence we used to force them and you couldn't just lower the gate and drop the pavement where it was, pooling on the driveway and into the fine, manicured green of the lawn. *This rich asshole would have a heart attack, shit himself, and die right here in front of the whole neighborhood. Not good for business. Not good at all.* We'd have to shovel it out. So Jack grabbed the asphalt lute, handed Lisa a smoothing blade and waved the two of us up on top and into the fumes and the stink. I remember the way things swam and ran: the greens and blues and whites of the suburbs, the red of Joey's Flannel, black of tar sloughing and calving like a glacier, the scrape of iron on iron, and curses echoing around the oven of the bed, and then the way one gull overhead split into two then three and those cries expanded in my chest flowering with heat, and how my body went boneless, slick, and sinewy, and I was flashing like a pike in a bucket emptied into a river that fed into an ocean with the whole sky dancing on its surface—a long thin muscle in flight. There's no moral to this. No takeaway except *sometimes you get so deep in the shit the only way out is to grab a shovel.* That's what Jack said anyway. One way to think of it. But long after we had scraped that truck-bed clean and he and Lisa had smoothed the driveway flat and black as the Mystic at night and I sat on a rich man's steps with my boot souls melted away as Joey retched on all fours by the tree-line, I took my first long drag from Lisa's cigarette. Neither fully in the shit nor out of it but high and flying and flowering, dizzy, as Jack slapped me on the back and laughed, and I took a long, deep breath, breathing the poison in.

You don't know shit about shit

she'd laughed, tilting back her head as I thought of Sarandon in that baseball movie only skinnier, sadder. That summer I spent fucking and sweating, hustling for cash and beer, working a long day in yards and on decks and deep in woods that needed greening, edging, weeding, clearing, heel to shovel, shuddered by the chainsaw's buzz, accumulating scratches, scars, and a brand new vocabulary. With the dropout and the washout, and the trust-fund kid whose dad wanted him to know what it was to work with his back. And the boss's sister, too old for me, too hard but pretty in the right light at the end of the day when everything glowed with exhaustion and "More Than A Feeling" floated up like a body through the static and the dashboard of the truck. She'd offer me a menthol cigarette that I would wave away, *no thanks*, eyes on the road, hands on the wheel, as she laughed at how young and stupid I was, how much I didn't know and had to learn and looked me up and down without heat but maybe just a little hunger and a little hate. Her life: my summer job. What she used to feed her kid and pay rent to her brother for the room above the garage: book-money. Weed money. Packs of condoms at the CVS. There was so much we didn't know, but what we did (or thought we did) we hung onto with both hands, climbed it rung by rung, fist over fist, telling ourselves, don't look down, keep going, don't stop, no matter how badly the shoulders ache or calves cramp, starving for blood.

Much
    For my son, Darius, at 18

How much? you used to ask when I came home from work and picked you up and spun you around and told you that I loved you. *How much?*

How much? we said, *how much? Whadda you want for it? C'mon.* Pointing at a baseball card or a Hershey Bar or Juice Box in the cafeteria. Or the cassette Matty made of an Aerosmith record. Then pretending to think about it. *Whadda you got?* A George Scott rookie card, a dollar fifty in loose change, . . . *how 'bout ten minutes alone with your sister?*

I got your mother, she's worth at least two bucks. Fuck you. Fuck off. How much we kept from our parents and how much they kept from us. And how much we hid from each other and ourselves and hid ourselves from each other. And big boys prowling the halls, *Hey Baby, Hey Honey, Hey little girl,*

How much? How much shit we talked and what we didn't talk about. *And what about those bruises on Billie's arms? And what happened to his mother? I haven't seen her in a while.* And the way Mr. Mitchell pulled our sisters to his lap, *c'mon, lets have a cuddle.* And *I won't have that kind of talk in this house, at this table. You just watch*

your mouth young man. And the cantors singing and the priest chanting in words that spoke of ancient vineyards and deserts and an old God I never knew but feared—God the father and the father as God, slamming the door as he left the house. God the mother—fierce and desperate with the love of all the Jewish and Catholic women who took me in their arms, insisting I stay for dinner then warned me not to date their daughters. And all their beautiful, wild daughters.

Too much man, too much. Of wood-fires burning through blizzards, and bonfires on Friday nights and the charred remains of Tony Testa's car in the junior high-school parking lot, set ablaze for the insurance, to pay for the coke he snorted on the bench in the locker room. And how much rage he played with. And how badly we lost. And the sour tang of gasoline. And the echo of the bullet entering Tony's brain, his father's service revolver dropping to his feet.

And how much silence surrounded that sound back then. And now. How much we tried to be—through twisted ankles and chipped teeth, and getting our bells rung and shaking it off and wobbling back onto the painted grass to the cheers of the crowd.

And copping a feel in darkened theaters, and hand-jobs in our parents' cars. How much we wanted what we were afraid of. And how much we were afraid of. The Russians and the bomb and AIDS and being called a homo and being associated with anyone who might be called one and *shit, what if I'm a homo? How do you know?*

And girls and how they seemed to move in packs and pointed and laughed and turned their backs, stealing glances at our glances, and our sisters slipping quietly into the house, makeup smeared and shirts untucked, faces flushed and trembling. How much we wanted to ask or say but closed our doors and went to bed and listened to them sobbing through the walls. And the videotape we passed around. And the magazines we found beneath the couch.

And could you drive me to the clinic? don't end up with your face on a Milk Carton. And *Just Say No.* And *it's 10 pm. Do you know where your children are?* They didn't. Not really. They didn't know us at all. And back then we all thought that that was what they wanted. Maybe

they were a little scared of us, how much we had to face, and how much we needed and how confused we were, how much damage was being done. All that was coming, coming at us, all at once. That no one could protect us from. And maybe it was all

Too much.

Barn-light

Red fox in barn-light. Windborne ash in the doorframe.
Starlings flap and shake the sky—a frosted blanket torn

from the line. Or a muscled pike winging its way

two feet beneath a skim of ice. All things holding fast
and loose. All seek shelter in flight.

II. INTO THE TEETH OF THE WIND

Jupiter, Desire, Hope

5/26/2020

we duck and cover   our mouths we carry   ourselves with us everywhere we are   **we go**   flames un   furled un   der the shadows of flags shuddering from heat rising we have been called   to account called home called   back from backyards and ballfields, boys and girls riding on our handlebars. Sometimes I think   we never left our childhood until   just   now. Sometimes I think we'll never emerge. And right now all I can think of are   bikes left tipped on their sides on basketball courts. Sometimes I wake in the night and swear I heard someone call my name but Rachael is asleep and the house is still and quiet. *Auditory hallucinations* Rachael says *everybody*   *has them* and I think of the time I woke in bed as a child and I swear I felt someone's hands around my neck and I couldn't scream and whoever it was   was laughing and to this day I don't know what it was I was hearing but I didn't imagine it and now it feels like   a pattern like things coming together like   all these threads were waiting to be pulled or   plucked like   this dark melody was always floating right in front   of me and around me and now we are all   entangled. I have read how slave-ship captains worked the taverns of Bristol, Swansea, Liverpool, paying off the barkeeps to run tabs all night long until   a sailor was both drunk and so far underwater he could never reach   the surface (if he could swim at all) and then, hit him with the bill and threats   of jail, and a raised wooden club. That's when the captain walked in the door with money to cover all debts   and a job. The worst in the world, carrying men and women by force across an ocean of disease and heat and fear, sharks following the wakes of ships with names like Jupiter,   Desire,   Hope. If 100 sailors left the port, 30 would come home. Hardened and full   of thirst. And so it was back to the bars. Some learned   to enjoy the work, make a life of it, with dreams of becoming   captain, maybe even own   the boat. Sailors, sometimes I think we are being woken   from our stupor, a club slapped to the polished wood. The debt   come due. And sure, there is always someone pulling on the strings, always someone further up the chains that we hear rattling. But we keep walking up the gangplank, telling ourselves we never had or have a choice. *Did you ever think this would happen in our lifetimes* Rachael asks me as we adjust our masks and cross the lot to the grocery store. *Yes* I hear myself respond, and almost hear the echo of laughter, feel my own hands tighten around my throat.

#naturalselection

After 21 drug-related homicides in under a year, Governor Jim Justice orders the WV National Guard into Huntington, WV

All week long the helicopters shuddered the sky above our city. East Side,
    West Side, Washington and Hal Greer Boulevard. Nose down
and predatory, low flying over "the Trap" and the 800 block and the
    Speedway by the University. And some looked up, and some
ducked, holding their arms above their heads like hostages. And some hid in
    their apartments beneath Formica countertops or in the basements
    and the bathrooms as if
there were an earthquake coming every time they heard a gunshot or a
    backfiring car. *We know
who they are* Governor Justice says, *and where and we will shut them down,
    lock them up.* Meanwhile

we lost 105 in 9 months. In five years 1700. Eight recovery beds for a
    thousand. Meanwhile
McKesson, Cardinal, Amerisource Bergen, made 400 billion in a year before
    the pills dried up. *But the problem
is the gangs from Detroit and who cares, let those bastards shoot each other.
    And let the druggies shoot themselves
up until they're gone. Load the heroine with Fentanyl and Fuck the Narcan
    anyway. It's called natural selection.* Meanwhile.
It is hard to keep the throat from tightening. So hard breathing through a
    straw. Staying calm
as the bullets hit the water two feet above your head. I had

a student and he was beautiful in that quiet way that takes you
    by surprise. He could reach you with his eyes without speaking. So you'd
    think that maybe
you'd really been seen for the first time, heard in a new way, blessed. And he
    could make
a guitar do almost anything and make words sing in their silences. But he had

   nerve pain and a limp. And maybe he was
a little too thin and sometimes he shook a bit like witch grass in the wind.
    But that was just Cool Chase, holding back
and leaning in, and who knew anyone or anything could take you suddenly
   that way before you knew what hit you. Like that morning

hurrying down the stairs and late for class, I pulled the heavy green door in
   and stepped into
an embrace. Someone else's child had wrapped his arms around my legs and
   hugged and would not go and the daycare teacher
laughed her nervous laugh and said. *I'm sorry. It's just Joey. He's like that.*
   And I bent and thought to pry him off and hurry on. But instead
lifted him (light, fragile as a seashell), and held on for a long moment, his
   heart throwing punches
against my chest, his breath at my ear, and I breathed his warmth and thought
   of my own son at that age after we lost
his mother and his brother and the many ways we clung

to each other and the teacher reached for him, looking around a little, frantic
   now, not knowing what to do or say, and I thought
of Chase on his back in that place he had to himself above his father's
   garage—the needle a few inches from his long
gentle fingers, froth at his lips as his lungs worked, desperate and drowning.
   And I heard a siren wail somewhere
and took my own little gasps, staring at this frightened woman, her arms
   outstretched, thinking of how we are always letting go, always
giving someone else's child away.

Night Patrol—Batavia Ohio

Who can resist an open door? You can't just shut it either. You need to be
    sure. Can't have the family come home from Christmas somewhere
in Vegas or the Hamptons to some strung-out kid on the couch or rabid dogs
    or skunks. Bats in the closets, frozen pipes. Not to mention theft.
    There's a reason you should use the deadbolts
on those chapel-style doors. So you stop; you climb the steps and look around
    and in. *Hello? Hello!*
I'm a police officer. An empty house at night is different, living. Not like a
    store past closing or a school. Or graveyard. You get those calls too.
Someone heard a noise, saw a shadow move. It is almost always nothing—
    an animal, a broken hinge on a door. Not always though. You have
    to go

through every room. Until you find yourself in someone else's basement, a
    revolver in your hand, with boxes, old computers and curtains, black
with mold. Even with the lights on shadows move. And what do you find?
KY on the bed-stand in a cereal bowl. A stack of bills. Leaves blown through
    the foyer with the wrappings of gifts. A stack of Jackie Collins
    novels. Half a bottle of Makers Mark. An empty bottle of sleeping
    pills—prescription. Nothing
really. And everything you shouldn't see or even know about. Knowing

is a lonely thing. You sit at the family table uninvited. You think, *maybe I
    should make some coffee, crack a beer. What the hell. Who would
    know?* But you don't. You leave.
You close the door
  behind you, tight as you can (you can't bolt it from the outside). Make a
    note to check back later on. But this time, stay out
of the basement and the bedrooms. Tomorrow you can file a report or wait
    until the family comes home and let them know, *You have to be*

more careful. Or maybe you will keep it to yourself—let them all believe that
        they were always safe, secure. That doors they shut
and lock stay closed, their basements free of mold—and lonely men
with guns. And all their secrets and their stories

stay their own.

America: Love It or Leave It

Man, you have a fucked up conception of love. A kind of one-in-the-
    morning-love that stands in the foyer, hand
on top of an open door, saying *Go on. You can leave any time you want to*
    while the kids pretend to sleep
upstairs and there's only one car in the driveway and the keys are in your
    pocket and everyone knows
there's a gun somewhere in the house with the safety off and it's as loaded as
    you are, stinking of booze,
and rage, thinking you're Brando in *Streetcar* when really, you're just another
    cracking-open-a-six-pack
-feet-up-watching-football-with-potato-chip-crumbs-in-his-navel kind of
    love asking *what's for dinner*
with his back to the kitchen saying, *I work hard all day and what do you do
    but sit your fat-ass on my couch*
and spend my money on worthless shit like (groceries, school-clothes, and
    the water bill). The *if-you've-got-*
nothing-to-hide-why-can't-you-give-me-your-passwords-search-history-cell-
    phone-bill kind of love that depends
on the other kind—the long and desperate staring past and out the door that
    thinks about just walking away, down
the sidewalk with the kids pleading from the bedroom windows and you
    screaming. *A where-would-I-even-go*
kind of love *and how far could I get* before the grabbing of an arm or fist-
    pull of hair from the roots. *After all*
these years and wasn't there a time when it was good? I'm sure there was.
    Before the babies and the bills, before
they closed the plant. Even now, sometimes, after all the curses and slapping
    of countertops and walls, and lights
going on and off throughout the house, and dust floating down from the
    ceiling. When the kids have finally fallen
back to sleep and you're on your knees on the other side of the bedroom or
    the bathroom door, begging *Baby baby*

please don't shut me out, I'll do, I'll say whatever you want me to when you
    know you'll be forgiven because you always
are and what are the choices. There is no out. There's only you and all your
    us and thems and either ors. And *that's right,*
I didn't think so's. Don't you know by now it's been a long, long time since
    this thing we have, had anything to do with love?

Burning Down The Cathedral

Sometimes we don't know exactly why we weep—a body language
    abstract and direct—fire-fighters struggle to control
the blaze—the ache of something awful carving into shadowed
    creases on the face
of sinner and saved—the same face the same body crowding as close
    as it can—miles away—the force
of heat pushing back—twin children edging to the stove—sensing
    how near a thing wonder comes

to dread—despair to

ecstasy—cataclysm—a silent unmouthed catechism—dangerous and
    brittle as
the martyr who—they say—walked miles holding his severed head in
    his hands—preaching
redemption—for weeks the citizens of Paris will breathe down their
    cathedral in a mist of lead and ash and holy
violence a hundred times beyond what is safe— some of them

have already begun transforming

into saints.

Catch and Release

Sometimes I struggle to forget myself in remembering what I've held and
    lost. The way
in calling for your touch, I am a body in the process of giving up the body as
    the fisherman entering a river
becomes the river. It is a near thing,

this casting. Releasing the right amount of line, to load the rod with weight
    and lift to leave
all surfaces behind so it can sing like a whip and take me with it, drawing
    back until I am a balancing act mid
-air, slack, then taut in the pull of what was, is, and comes: line and load
    where things unfurl, unfold, so the lure that licks the air flies, floats
down soft to rest trembling on the skin of another world like a hand to the
    back
of a lover, and there are so many worlds shimmering, layered one
upon another. It takes an awful kind of gentleness, letting go while holding to
the line that links them, links me to

    the many men I've been, the hands I've held, arms that took me in for a night, a day, a year, ten, too many long and lonely silences, beds I've wrecked, and cars, a marriage, flights I've taken over every continent, flights I missed, and meetings too, chances, the job I didn't take at the charter school in Michigan, jobs I took that damned near killed me, paving driveways, cleaning toilets, treework, brickwork, selling sneakers at the mall, each kiss, some sad, some desperate, some sweet with bourbon, too many bourbons ordered neat in too many bars, the many songs I've played and sung with too many lead guitarists, too many love poems and far,

    far too many elegies. Two sons. Two wives. Two lives converging at a trembling point. Searching

for equilibrium the way a man might stare at sun's first crescent on a river at
    dawn when he can still feel the halo of the moon and is stretched
like a shadow across a hundred feet of moving water, and the cold slows
    down the heart until he hears it in the cisterns

and the ventricles thump close as the bracken fern and muck dissolve into
    a fine mist rising with the swept back wings of a northern harrier
    reflected on the surface. Under it,

a single muscle moving in a field of flow, a pattern self-contained and
    undulant that waves us forward by flexing
back and upward through shafts and globes until we are caught and pulled

thrashing from this world. I wonder if my son was listening as I whispered
    breathe in, breathe out, relax I've got you, then slipped a hand away
    from the hollow of his back as he

arced up, arms spread, eyes encircled in watery light and shot with terror,
    flickering from me to something
in the sky, a dragonfly, or a bird, or the sun in its slow blinding course. Or
    was he beyond
listening. Beyond the spell of words as he
balanced there on the edge of panic, of joy. And what did he see if he saw
    at all as I backed away
in awe or was it just the inward staring wide-eyed shock of birth?

Sometimes I'd Forget

Now my charms are all o'erthrown,
And what strength I have's mine own,
Which is most faint.

You were a child. Only four and painted into bright blue and yellow
	spongebob squarepants pajamas,
so tight they formed a second skin and I watched you watch snowflakes
	descend, marveling
at how much they seemed like floating ash. Burning your lips and tongue on
	cocoa and a slowly dissolving
scoop of fluff. When all you wanted was to throw on snow pants, pull in the
	heavy door
and sled down from our little cell at the top of the mountain. Back then,
	maybe I was reconciled
as we performed whatever normal was. Pretending I could be a mother and
	a brother to you—and you,
a little boy, my son. Sometimes you would cry in the bathtub for no reason
	at all, saying *I'm lonely.*
And I'd say nothing. What is there to say? Their names unsayable, a conjuring
	that risked turning me into
something awful, ugly, dark. And if I spoke, if I spoke at all, I'd change the
	subject, or start
singing, *row row row your boat*, or say *that's OK Bear, sometimes we all get
	lonely* and I'd scrub
your back. And when I put you to sleep it was like taking off a mask. That
	was when I
scared myself the most. Staring into mirrors as if they could say the future.
	As if they could tell me something

I wanted to know. Didn't already know. How crazy is this love and rage that
	pulls us out
and forward while holding us to the past? Leaving us stranded at the ends of
	stories then asking us

to begin? You deserved so much
more than what we had. Two monks by dawn-light staggering,
trembling into the teeth of the wind.

In the moment where I decide there must be a God because
  --For Rachael

I've learned to move in shadows where She keeps her secrets hidden—though She
    won't tell
or show them. Everything's an arching brow, a romp, a wink. Sacred words can form
    a spell. But it's a privilege
to know them. And a game. There is a scar, a crescent by your eye that makes me
    want to climb into it. And make a temple there and do
nothing but chant your name. Though this God would kick my columns down. And
    set the sanctuary to blaze. She craves a different kind of music. Who gives

anyone the right to make of you a door, a hallway and pass through you. Or stay
    there to whisper every prayer of thanks he knows. God knows
    She goes everywhere and only where She wants to
and so do you. You float a hand along my back or press it downward on my chest to
    crack it open. And laugh, giggle, arch your spine. To give
and take a kind of absolution. Consumption all consuming. Crazy with the
    movement, such a freak, a naked dancer in broad daylight through the
    crowded city streets. A singer who keeps changing
the melody, the key, and tempo, every time we think we've caught

the tune and try to sing it with you. And the sounds you make can shake the
    headboards of every house on 7th Avenue (and the floorboards
too—and rattle the roofs). And sometimes I can hear the planet howl like caves with
    rivers pouring through them. Aching with violets and violence that flowers
    like a space
or time and folds itself into itself again, again—a throbbing susurration. A latent

explosion. And faith that even if there were no God we could from this

    make one to worship.

Wow! Signal: Dredging Light
I too am not a bit tamed—I too am untranslatable—Walt Whitman

When it comes, it finds me shin-deep in our creek as I bend my knees, lock
    elbows and strain to dig down and in, and
lift the tall grass from the water, heavy, sucking free the silt and sod and
    sediment, so when the storms of April arrive, the waters will not flood
my lawn and threaten the foundation of my home. Summer,
when everything sings and stings with its need to be
uncontained, and penetrate the skin. And I am

at once the man with the bad hip and clicking shoulder and
the teenager working for the landscaping company, his flannel caught on a
    branch as it dives into the chipper. And I am
screaming and spinning out of the shirt, away from the blades. And I am
a boy watching in wonder, his mother lift and turn and stretch across a high
    school stage in white tights and slippers, my sisters on either side, their
    long, thin backs growing wings,
becoming birds that glide over the water, casting shadows that chase each
    other down the beach as I shout after them. *Slow down. Wait*
for me. And the hound howling for hours through the steam of evening from
    behind the gate of the neighbors yard, straining at his leash. And

the sod, and the silt, and the grass—my hair as wet and heavy as the nearly
    drowned. But come back, gasping. Everything insisting I am
not confined in these yellow waders or this body or this creek. And the
    shovel

is not a shovel but a dish, glittering with stars which are the future and the
    past at once, sending their messages of birth and burial. Ear to the rail,
    cheekbone to the track, I receive, picking up vibrations that dance
    across the distances

and through the skull to the tongue with a tang of pomegranates reddening
	the lips: somewhere on the burning

sand of an ever expanding beach, unmodulated waves that might have come
	from a light-house beacon somewhere in the constellation of
	Sagittarius strain

at full draw aiming arrows across the heavens, flash and turn, turn

and flash. Somewhere in Ohio the astronomer shot through
with wonder stares at a signal he's been waiting for without hope and
	desperate with need, works out the coordinates, searching for the
	source of what he sees. A message

undecodable can say anything, everything. Old gods, sing

the language of the sumac reaching for the water pipes beneath the
	basement, curled around the metal, tightening its grip

or how the starlings wheel in a single wave, a wing.
Play the notes in any sequence. I am feathered with your arrows. I am wading
	in the waters. I am dredging my creek
come down from the mountains, staggering
with light and heat.

Acknowledgements

Grateful acknowledgement is given to the magazines and anthologies where many of these poems were originally printed, sometimes in slightly different forms. As always, thanks are always given to the many friends and family who have read these poems in earlier versions and provided

The 64 Best Poets of 2019 (Black Mountain Press): "The Tongue is a fire," "Much"

The American Journal of Poetry: "#naturalselection" and "On Hearing a Scream Outside My Window"

Constellations: "Sometimes I'd Forget"

Flock: "Catch and Release"

The James Dickey Review: "Night Patrol: Batavia Ohio"

Jelly Bucket: "Warning Signs"

The MacGuffin: "Barn-light"

Mud Season: "Wow! Signal: Dredging Light" and "The Tongue is a Fire"

The Northhampton Review (UK): "Redemption Center"

Prime Number Magazine: "Jupiter, Desire, Hope"

The Raw Art Review: "Some Crazy-Ass Shit," "You Don't Know Shit about Shit," "Pavement," "Burning Down the Cathedral," "In the moment where I decide there must be a God because," and "Donnie Russo and the Huffy Pro Thunder"

The Rise-Up Review: "America: Love It Or Leave It"

Praise for Much

"It is no small thing, this casting," Joel Peckham writes of fishing, but it might be any action described in this book. Whether these characters and speakers are shoveling asphalt, trying and failing to pop a wheelie, or engaged in contentious flirtation, they are fully aware both of their unredeemed bodies and the horizons the spirit senses but can only aspire to. In long, sinewy lines or flowing prose poems, Peckham casts a loving but unsentimenal gaze over his subjects. Here is a poet who writes with the eye of a seer, one whose lines arouse the lyric fury available only to those poets who have thoroughly mastered their craft.

Al Maginnes, Author of *Sleeping Through the Graveyard Shift*

Gaston Bachelard once wrote that "An excess of childhood is the germ of a poem"--and in Joel Peckham, Jr.'s miraculous jewel of a book such excess is embraced wildly, ferociously, and with such teeming love of life and memory it trickles over into eternity. In poem after poem and in lyrical prose his line "All seek shelter in flight" reminds us that the human soul is meant for soaring. Astonishing.

Robert Vivian, Author of *All I Feel is Rivers: Dervish Essays*

Biography

 **Joel Peckham, Jr.** has published seven books of poetry and nonfiction, most recently *God's Bicycle* and *Body Memory*. Individual poems have appeared recently in or are forthcoming in *Prairie Schooner, The Southern Review, The Sugar House Review, Cave Wall, The Beloit Poetry Journal* and many others. Currently he is editing an anthology of ecstatic poetry for New Rivers Press, titled *Wild Gods: The Ecstatic in American Poetry and Prose*. His newest collection, *Bone Music,* is forthcoming in 2021 from Stephen F. Austin University Press. He is an Associate Professor of English Literature at Marshall University where he teaches a broad range of courses in Creative Writing and American Literature. He lives in Huntington West Virginia with his wife, Rachael and son Darius, both accomplished poets and essayists.